HOW TO BE A
PARLIAMENTARIAN

(A GUIDE FOR ALL
ASPIRING PARLIAMENTARIANS)

Second Edition

By M. Eugene Bierbaum, Ph.D., CPP-T

With Foreword by Nancy Sylvester, M.A., CPP-T

American Institute of Parliamentarians
Education Department
2014

© 2014 by the American Institute of Parliamentarians
www.aipparl.org
aip@aipparl.org
888.664.0428

Printed in the United States of America
Second Edition ISBN: 978-0-942736-34-2
Second Edition, First Printing, June 2014
1 2 3 4 5 6 7 8 9 10

The AIP Education Department expresses great appreciation to Ann L. Rempel, CPP-T, for editing the second edition of this book. The department also thanks Kay Crews, CP, who handled all formatting issues with patience and precision in producing this edition.

Published by the
Education Department
American Institute of Parliamentarians
Jeanette N. Williams, CP-T, Education Director
Ann L. Rempel, CPP-T, Printed Materials Division Chair
Alison Wallis, JD, CP-T, President

Foreword

This book continues to be a great follow up to Dr. Bierbaum's "presiding" book. Again, the emphasis is on teamwork and the flow of communication between the presiding officer and the parliamentarian, but this book views the process from the perspective of the aspiring parliamentarian.

While being a professional parliamentarian is an exciting and rewarding profession, there is not a clearly defined curriculum to study to become one. Most professional parliamentarians have learned through trial and error and by relying on other parliamentarians.

This book is a useful guide for anyone considering entering the parliamentary profession. The candidate is first asked to indulge in self-analysis, and consider whether he or she really wants to be a parliamentarian. Dr. Bierbaum then leads the novice through a logical sequence of study and preparation, finding jobs, working with a team, earning credentials, dealing with clients, and survival techniques in the profession.

This book is useful both to those who plan to earn credentials and become professional parliamentarians, and to those who wish to serve as a "member parliamentarian" of one organization. Recognizing that the great majority of parliamentarians are members of the group that they serve, special attention is given to the requirements and needs of the member parliamentarian.

This is not a book on parliamentary procedure. Rather, it is a survival guide for those who wish to enter the parliamentary profession. It "fills in the blanks" of the leading parliamentary authorities which generally devote only a few pages to the position of parliamentarian.

I highly recommend this book to anyone who is planning to serve as a parliamentarian. Here you will find a detailed job description for the role of parliamentarian, and an in-depth analysis of the many ways in which a parliamentarian communicates with presiding officers, client organizations, and the profession as a whole. My favorite chapter is the last chapter because it reminds the reader that we must give back to our profession in order for our profession to flourish. Dr. Bierbaum has spent his entire career living the principles expressed in that chapter!

Nancy Sylvester, CPP-T, PRP

M. Eugene Bierbaum received his Ph.D. in communication theory from the University of Missouri in 1965 and served as the tenth president of AIP during 1976-1978. During 1979-1983 he served as curriculum director for the first AIP Practicums offered at the College of William and Mary. He served as accrediting director during 1981-1984 and education director during 1997-2000. Following twenty-five years of teaching communication studies at the State University of New York, he retired in 1992 with the title of professor emeritus. During 1991-2001 he chaired a committee to write the Joint Code of Ethics that was subsequently adopted by the American Institute of Parliamentarians and the National Association of Parliamentarians. He continues to teach workshops on parliamentary procedure throughout the United States.

Introduction

WARNING:
THIS BOOK WILL TEACH YOU NOTHING
ABOUT PARLIAMENTARY PROCEDURE!

The above warning should not be necessary. The title *How to be a Parliamentarian* tells you what this book is about. Obviously, you will need to study parliamentary procedure and learn the rules. This book, however, is not about the rules; it is about how you structure your training and how you prepare for the unique position of "parliamentarian."

Some clubs have made the mistake of appointing any member as parliamentarian, and then providing that person with no training. Even if the person makes a reasonable effort to learn the rules, this person is often not suited to the job. A past president, for example, who has taken strong positions on many controversial issues, may be unable to fulfill the role of parliamentarian.

The first two chapters of this book will help you decide whether you are naturally suited to the role of parliamentarian and whether this is something that you really want to do. Chapter 3 provides guidelines for starting your parliamentary education, and Chapter 4 gives advice on selecting your first jobs. Chapters 5-8 explain the work of the parliamentarian in detail, from the initial preparation prior to meetings to the follow-up actions that should be taken after each meeting. Chapters 9-11 are written for those who wish to move up to the rank of professional parliamentarian, serving many varieties of clients, traveling extensively, and often commanding huge fees.

Any person wishing to serve as parliamentarian at any level will find something of value in this book. You will master the tools of your trade, learn how to function as a member of a presiding team, and learn new methods of communicating during meetings. The only thing you won't learn here is "parliamentary procedure."

This page intentionally left blank.

Contents

This page intentionally left blank.

Chapter 1
Can You Be a Parliamentarian?

Not everyone is well suited to be a parliamentarian. Some will perform much better than others in this role because of background, temperament, and disposition. Before agreeing to serve as a parliamentarian, or even before attempting to train yourself for this role, here are some questions that you should ask yourself.

1. Am I a "detail" person?

2. Does organization matter in my life?

3. Do I willingly abide by the rules?

4. Can I see more than one side of most issues?

5. Can I tolerate long meetings?

6. Do I have good writing and oral communication skills?

7. Am I comfortable with technology?

8. Do I enjoy traveling?

Before turning to the next page, answer yes or no to each of the above questions. Answer honestly, and don't "cheat" by looking ahead to the next page. This short quiz, more than anything else will help you determine whether you should even consider being a parliamentarian.

Your Answers:

1. _____

2. _____

3. _____

4. _____

5. _____

6. _____

7. _____

8. _____

A good prospect for the role of parliamentarian would likely answer "yes" to at least six of the eight questions. But how you answered may have depended at least partly on how you interpreted the question. We'll discuss and elaborate on each of the eight questions and, if you find that you misinterpreted a question, you are allowed to go back and change your answer. Now let's look at each question and examine some of the factors that may have influenced your answer.

1.   Am I a "detail" person?

Are you the type of person who pays attention to details in your life? Are you careful about dressing appropriately for various formal and informal occasions? Do you regularly balance your checkbook? Do you reply to all of your mail that requires a reply? Do you willingly keep written records?

Everyone differs, of course, in the amount of attention that he gives to the details that surround your life. In general, however, parliamentarians do attend to details more than others. They will spend a great deal of time, for example, deciding whether one particular word belongs in a set of bylaws. They will need to spend considerable time deciding whether a given word should be "must," "shall," "should," "may," or some other word. If you are not willing to devote time to details, you probably should not be a parliamentarian.

2.   Does organization matter in my life?

If you have a desk where you work regularly, how does your desk look? If you have a file cabinet, are your files neatly organized so that you can find things quickly? If you cook, are your recipes filed neatly so that you can quickly locate a recipe that you haven't used for years? When you write letters, do you neatly dispose of each topic before moving on to the next, or do your letters tend to "ramble"? Throughout your house, do you have a place for each thing you own, and everything neatly in its place?

Again, everyone differs in the degree to which they organize their lives. And some degree of disorganization may be desirable, particularly when it comes to entertainment and social life. In general, however, parliamentarians tend to be highly organized individuals. They keep libraries and files of documents pertaining to many different organizations. They carry around brief cases full of scripts, books, correspondence, meeting agendas, rules, and other key documents. In any situation, they must be able to locate key documents quickly. Without a good sense of organization, it is unlikely that you can function effectively as a parliamentarian.

3. Do I willingly abide by the rules?

You may have looked at this question and wondered what *rules* were being referred to. Rules have many names. Depending on where the rules come from, they may be referred to as laws (the rules of society that govern all of us), contracts (rules that we voluntarily agree to by signing a document), customs or traditions (the unspoken and often unwritten rules that govern how we relate to people around us) or other terminology. Regardless of where the rule came from, it always refers to a boundary of some sort, and you have a choice of whether to stay within that boundary or break the rule.

During most of your life, have you been willing to operate within the boundaries prescribed by society? When driving, do you obey the rules of the road? When you sign a rental lease, do you obey the terms of the lease? Do you normally pay your bills on time? When you want to reach a goal, do you generally "play by the rules" or do you tend to "step on people" to get where you want to be?

Parliamentarians spend a substantial part of their life writing, interpreting, and helping to enforce rules. If most of your life has been spent operating outside the boundaries established by society, you might find it difficult to serve as a parliamentarian. Rules should be an important part of your life. Parliamentarians almost always operate in an environment in which members are expected to follow the rules. Following the rules is a lifelong orientation that is not easily changed, and living within prescribed boundaries should be an integral part of your life before you even consider becoming a parliamentarian.

4. Can I see more than one side of most issues?

When confronted with a controversial issue, do you tend to see only the "right" side of the issue, or can you broaden your perspective to include more than one possible viewpoint? Do you view issues in terms of "black and white," (i.e., right and wrong) or can you often see varying shades of "gray"?

When you practice as a parliamentarian, you will often be in the middle of highly controversial issues. Various factions may come to you for advice, each faction believing that it has the right answer or solution to a problem. Your work as a parliamentarian will be easier and more productive if you can view a given controversy from several different perspectives. Often there is no right or wrong answer to a problem, only a variety of approaches to solving the problem.

5. Can I tolerate long meetings?

"Tolerate" has more than one meaning. You must be able to tolerate the boredom of lengthy reports that contain no specific recommendations for action. You must be able to stay awake and alert during tedious, lengthy, and sometimes rambling speeches. You must also tolerate the stress of lengthy, highly emotional meetings where competing factions have a great deal at stake. Meetings may start as early as 6 a.m. or as late as midnight, and can drag on for hours.

You must also be physically tolerant of long meetings. Some people cannot sit for extended periods of time due to lower back problems. Others are prone to develop migraine headaches or need frequent medication. If you have any physical, mental, or emotional impairment that makes it difficult for you to withstand the stress of lengthy meetings, you may not be a strong candidate for the position of parliamentarian.

6. Do I have good writing and oral communication skills?

You will frequently be called on to give opinions and advice, both in writing and orally. Your ability to communicate well is therefore critical to your success as a parliamentarian. You must be able to do research on a complex procedural matter and state your findings clearly. Any hint of ambiguity or lack of clarity on a key issue can be devastating to an organization.

If you have problems with written or oral communication, you should consider taking college level courses in areas of weakness. Courses in writing, public speaking, interpersonal communication, and organizational communication can be major assets for the professional parliamentarian.

7.   Am I comfortable with technology?

Technology is constantly changing, and some people adjust to new technologies much more quickly than others. You need not be an expert in the latest technological advances, but you must be willing to take the time to master any technology that will be helpful to your parliamentary work. Much of your parliamentary advice will be transmitted through the latest technology. Organizations are constantly experimenting with new methods of holding conferences and new voting systems. You may also be expected to use technology when teaching parliamentary workshops.

If you are willing to make the effort to keep up with technological changes, you will be fine. Too much timidity in this area, however, can impede the work of a parliamentarian.

8.   Do I enjoy traveling?

Are you the type of person who feels safe and secure only when comfortably snuggled in your own bed at home? Do you dread travel to new destinations? Do you dislike the confusion and bustle of staying in large hotels? Are you tolerant of the chaos surrounding airports, taxis and limousines?

If you are content to function locally as a parliamentarian, you probably need not be concerned about travel. Professional parliamentarians, however, travel extensively. Expect to travel lengthy distances every time you interview for a new position, teach a workshop, or serve as parliamentarian for a convention, conference, or board meeting. You will be happier in your work if you enjoy traveling and meeting new people.

Relatively few people make a perfect score on the above quiz by answering "yes" to every question. The best candidates for the position, however, are likely to answer affirmatively on at least six of the eight questions. If, after reviewing this list of questions, you are convinced that you are not a good candidate for parliamentarian, you should find another role in which you are more comfortable. Large organizations hire many kinds of consultants and specialists. Develop expertise in areas that you will be comfortable and function effectively.

Chapter 2
Do You Want To Be a Parliamentarian?

If you passed the quiz in Chapter 1 with a grade of at least 6 out of 8, you are now reasonably certain that you have the capability to become a parliamentarian. The next question, however, is whether you really want this job. In this chapter, we will look at some of the common expectations of novice parliamentarians, and then compare the reality with the expectation. What is it that you really want and expect from your clients and from the parliamentary profession? Are your expectations realistic or idealistic? If you come into the profession for the wrong reasons, you may experience disappointment and failure very early in your career. Let's take a look at some of the most common expectations of novice parliamentarians.

Expectations of the Novice Parliamentarian

Expectation #1: "I want to be the 'star' of the show!"

It's surprising how many novice parliamentarians enter the profession expecting to be at the very center of attention throughout their careers. They somehow fail to grasp that they are in training to be a consultant, not a CEO. They often make the mistake of attempting to put themselves on an even level with the elected officers of the organization. This is a big mistake. The elected officers have a mandate to act on behalf of the membership; you do not. You provide expertise in one key area, rules and procedures.

To make matters worse, some parliamentarians are treated as "stars" by their early clients, and thus become accustomed to a level of attention that cannot be sustained throughout one's professional career. Some organizations do tend to elevate their parliamentarians to a higher status than is usual for a consultant. Enjoy it, but don't get used to it. Sooner or later you will confront the reality that the executive director, the president, and other officers regard you as a consultant and advisor. You are only one of many consultants and organizational specialists.

Novice parliamentarians often need to develop a little humility to perform effectively. Learn to play a secondary role, and play it well. If you do your job, which is to make the meeting run smoothly, you will likely receive some credit for a job well done. But you should realize at the outset that many others will receive equal credit. Executive directors, convention co-ordinators, media specialists, consulting attorneys, and many other specialists will share the spotlight with you, and may often "steal the show." It is vitally important to your career that you be willing to acknowledge the contributions made by many other specialists who know little or nothing about parliamentary procedure.

The key word for you to focus on early in your career is the word "serve." You are hired to serve an organization. Your service extends beyond the president to include other officers, the board of directors, key committees, and individual factions and members. The exact nature of your service will vary from one organization to another, but your central focus is always to keep the business of the organization flowing smoothly.

Expectation #2: "I want to preside."

Novice parliamentarians often spend a great deal of class time practicing how to preside over meetings. Some of them, unfortunately, seem to expect that this is how they will spend their time as professional parliamentarians. To be sure, some professional parliamentarians with specialized training have become expert presiders. They are hired by groups for special meetings such as adopting a revision of the bylaws, considering a major dues increase, or changing the membership categories. A few are hired over long periods of time, but these are the exception, not the rule.

Parliamentarians must understand that their job responsibility is the direct opposite of the elected presiding officer. The presiding officer is elected from inside the organization and functions as the organization's expert on matters of membership and organizational issues and goals. The parliamentarian should normally be appointed from outside the membership. This person's expertise is in procedural matters.

Any parliamentarian, whether hired in the usual advisory capacity or to preside, functions primarily as a procedural expert. Presiding parliamentarians should receive special training as presiders. A novice entering the profession should recognize from the outset that he or she will likely spend little if any time presiding. The inherent role of a parliamentarian is that of consultant and advisor.

Expectation #3: "I want to make lots of money."

Novice parliamentarians often begin their work with inflated ideas of charging large fees. There is nothing unethical about this since the client, and only the client, decides the true worth of any consultant. Realistically, however, parliamentarians lacking experience with national and international organizations do not command large fees during their first year or two. Be prepared to work for local groups for very low fees when you first begin to practice. You may even want to serve without a fee for the purpose of gaining experience. Keep in mind, however, that the amount and quality of the work expected has little or no relation to your fee. Every organization will expect quality work from you even if you serve without pay.

As you gain experience, you will gradually raise your fee schedule. You will know that you are near the top of your profession when you are hired by a national or international organization that is restructuring, revising its bylaws, or making substantial changes in its dues or membership structure. Chapter 8 will discuss the question of fee schedules in more detail.

What a Parliamentarian Is Not

In addition to cultivating realistic expectations, the novice parliamentarian should also have clear understanding of what a parliamentarian is not. Your successful performance as a parliamentarian depends partly on a clear understanding of certain roles that are not appropriate for any parliamentarian.

A parliamentarian is not a voting member.

Parliamentarians are normally hired from outside the organization and therefore have no membership rights. They have no right to be notified of meetings, to attend meetings, to speak on issues, or to vote. They are paid consultants, brought in from the outside to function as procedural experts.

Some organizations use their own members as parliamentarians, primarily because they lack the necessary funding to bring in an outside parliamentarian. If you should ever serve as a member parliamentarian, remember that you must give up most of your normal membership rights at the time of your appointment as parliamentarian. You still have the right to be notified of meetings and to attend meetings, but, under most circumstances, you may not speak to issues or vote.

In some respects, the member parliamentarian is more restricted than the presiding officer. The presiding officer retains the right to vacate the chair, and then to speak and vote as any other member while out of the chair. The parliamentarian has no such right. The parliamentarian may never speak to a substantive issue, and may vote only if the vote is taken by secret ballot. The presiding officer may cast a deciding vote whenever the vote is close; the parliamentarian may not.

Whether you are a professional parliamentarian hired from outside the organization or a member parliamentarian, your position as parliamentarian is the same. You are a consultant and advisor, and you cannot abandon or alter this role during any meeting that you serve as parliamentarian.

A parliamentarian is not an advocate or an interested party.

You should not accept an appointment as parliamentarian for any meeting in which you have a vested interest in the outcome. If you, as a member parliamentarian, have strong feelings about some of the issues to come before the assembly, you must keep your private views to yourself. You may never be an advocate, nor may you manipulate procedures for the purpose of attaining a specific outcome. Your job is to ensure that procedures are followed correctly without regard to the outcome.

A parliamentarian is not "window dressing."

Some organizations tend to hire parliamentarians primarily to provide the appearance of fairness, thus providing "window dressing" for procedure that may be unethical and basically unfair to the membership. Any parliamentarian who suspects such tactics should decline to accept the appointment. Parliamentarians cannot afford to be manipulated to serve the ends of a particular presiding officer, executive director, or board of directors. If, during a meeting, you perceive that your advice is being ignored and that your presence is helping to legitimize unfair proceedings, you should make clear that you will resign immediately at the close of the meeting.

If you have carefully considered all of the above factors, you should now be in a position to decide if you really want to be a parliamentarian. If you are still with us, read on.

This page intentionally left blank.

Chapter 3
Care and Feeding of the Novice

Since you reached this point and are still reading, you must have some predisposition toward the role of parliamentarian. Now the question arises, how shall you obtain the necessary education and training to serve as a parliamentarian? Unfortunately, many people believe that the only prerequisite is to go the library, check out some edition of *Robert's Rules*, read it, and you're ready to go. No, it's not quite that simple.

First of all, you need to decide which parliamentary authority you want to study. Many editions of *Robert's Rules* are available in bookstores and libraries throughout the country, and you need to know where to start. Many parliamentarians have chosen not to start with *Robert's Rules*. Books of rules for running meetings are known as "parliamentary authorities," and you have many choices available to you other than *Robert's Rules of Order Newly Revised*. One favorite choice for beginning parliamentarians is *American Institute of Parliamentarians Standard Code of Parliamentary Procedure*. Other choices include *Demeter's Manual of Parliamentary Law and Procedure* and *Cannon's Concise Guide to Rules of Order*. (See the page 63 of this book for references cited.)

Indeed, you have several key decisions facing you as you enter the parliamentary profession, and your choices at this early stage will likely affect your entire professional career. Let's discuss some of the choices that you must make before you even open one of the parliamentary authorities for study.

Choosing a Parliamentary Authority

Your first choice is whether to study a single parliamentary authority or whether to study several parliamentary authorities simultaneously. Any of the above-mentioned parliamentary authorities would be a good choice for a beginner who wishes to study only one book at a time. A very different approach is utilized in a book entitled *Fundamentals of Parliamentary Law and Procedure*, Fourth Edition. The lessons in this book contain reading assignments from several different parliamentary authorities.

You will need to decide whether you wish to focus only on one parliamentary authority during the early stages of your training, or whether you wish to use the multiple authority approach embodied in the *Fundamentals* text. Either approach will work, as long as you apply yourself and are willing to spend several hours per week in serious study.

If you choose the multiple authority approach, probably your best place to begin is with the *Fundamentals of Parliamentary Law and Procedure* text. The lessons in the book contain reading assignments from four well known parliamentary authorities: *Robert's Rules of Order Newly Revised, American Institute of Parliamentarians Standard Code of Parliamentary Procedure, Demeter's Manual of Parliamentary Law and Procedure,* and *Riddick's Rules of Procedure.*

Many beginning students of parliamentary procedure have used the single authority approach simply because the only book they have ever heard of related to parliamentary procedure is *Robert's Rules.* If you decide on this approach, however, it is important that, once you have mastered your first authority, you move on to study other parliamentary authorities. You will never master the underlying principles of parliamentary procedure if you limit your study to one book. Most professional parliamentarians have complete home libraries of parliamentary authorities and other documents which they consult frequently.

Most parliamentarians who begin their studies from a single parliamentary authority choose the current edition of either *Robert's Rules of Order Newly Revised* or *American Institute of Parliamentarians Standard Code of Parliamentary Procedure.* Regardless of which authority you choose, be sure that you have the current edition since this is the edition that your clients will be using.

The main advantage of choosing *Robert's Rules of Order Newly Revised* as a beginning point is that this is the authority required by most bylaws of voluntary associations. The disadvantage is that this authority is laden with technical jargon and complex rules. If you try to master parliamentary procedure by reading this book through from beginning to end, you will probably fail. This book is written primarily as a reference manual (i.e., a way to look up answers to specific questions), not a beginning-level textbook.

The main advantage of choosing *American Institute of Parliamentarians Standard Code of Parliamentary Procedure* is that it is much more readable. It is written in language that beginners can understand, and many of its rules have been simplified. For example, *Robert's Rules* contains lists of many kinds of motions that can be reconsidered whereas *AIP Standard Code* permits only the main motion to be reconsidered. A possible disadvantage of starting with *AIP Standard Code* is that you might become "spoiled" with the readable language of the book and then have trouble moving to the more complex terminology of *Robert's Rules*.

Regardless of which way you choose to start, you will probably want to incorporate both *Robert's Rules* and *AIP Standard Code* into your early training. After your first year or two in the profession, you should study at least two more authorities so that you begin to get the "feel" of the profession as a whole, not just one book.

Beginning Formal Studies

Selecting a parliamentary authority (or authorities) as a beginning point for your studies is only the first step in your training. Now you need to decide how you will be trained. The poorest choice is to try to do this "on your own" with no supervision. True, there are many self-taught parliamentarians in the field, but most of them wish that they had started with a more formal approach to their education.

The simple fact is that parliamentary procedure cannot be learned from a book any more than you can master a foreign language by reading a book. To learn parliamentary procedure, you need to learn more than just rules. You also need to learn how to "speak the language" and this requires you to interact with other people. Parliamentary procedure, by its very nature, is interactive. You could read many books and memorize endless lists of rules and still not be very conversant in a live meeting situation.

The best approach, by far, is to attend workshops, practicums, and seminars that involve interactive training for beginners. These are available at many levels through the American Institute of Parliamentarians (AIP), which offers at least two practicums each year. One practicum is held on the west coast, usually in late January, and one is held on the east coast, usually in June. Information about practicums is available on the AIP website. Educational workshops are also taught in connection with AIP's Annual Session and in chapter meetings.

Another choice is to locate courses and workshops offered in your immediate geographical area. Many colleges and universities offer courses in parliamentary procedure, either as part of their communication studies program or through their continuing education program. You could contact AIP directly to find out if there is a local chapter in your area that offers educational workshops.

Another choice that has been effectively utilized by many beginners is to learn parliamentary procedure by correspondence. AIP offers several correspondence courses, and each course is taught by a certified parliamentarian or a certified professional parliamentarian. These courses contain more than reading assignments. They provide opportunities to interact with your instructor and to ensure that your early mistakes are corrected quickly and effectively.

The choice of where to begin is yours; the important thing is to begin. Choose your parliamentary authority (or authorities) carefully and plan for lots of interaction, either in live meeting situations or by correspondence, early in your training. Within the first year of your training, you will begin to get a "feel" for what parliamentary procedure is all about and you will want to move as quickly as you can to become a practitioner in the field.

Build Your Personal Library

Your library probably begins the latest available editions of *Robert's Rules of Order Newly Revised*, *American Institute of Parliamentarians Standard Code of Parliamentary Procedure*, and *Fundamentals of Parliamentary Law and Procedure*. These books, however, are only the beginning of what will eventually become your own personal library. You will certainly want to add several more parliamentary authorities. You should own and be familiar with the content of at least two of the following which are sold by AIP:

- *Cannon's Concise Guide to Rules of Order*

- *Demeter's Manual of Parliamentary Law and Procedure*

- *Readings in Parliamentary Law*

- *Riddick's Rules of Procedure*

As you become more experienced, you will eventually add volumes dealing with parliamentary procedure for conventions, church organizations, condominium and homeowner associations, and many other types of specialty organizations.

Your library will not be limited to books. Other library acquisitions may include:

- State codes, corporation codes, and codes for nonprofit corporations.

- Sample certificates of incorporation.

- Sample bylaws for various types of organizations.

- Instructional audio and video tapes.

One of the most important additions to your library will be delivered to your doorstep quarterly if you are a member of AIP. The *Parliamentary Journal*, which is included with your membership, provides up-to-date articles on many aspects of parliamentary procedure as well as the latest developments in the profession.

Join the Profession

You should, at an early stage in your career, join one or more of the parliamentary organizations that have strong credentialing programs for aspiring parliamentarians.

The American Institute of Parliamentarians (AIP) provides an excellent entry point. You can contact AIP directly at www.aipparl.org or by simply calling the headquarters office at 888-664-0428. Ask for a membership application and a list of materials for sale. Your membership in AIP will quickly bring publications to your doorstep to provide information about workshops, practicums, and seminars to further your parliamentary education.

You need not seek credentials immediately, but, after having mastered the basics of the profession, you will want to obtain some formal recognition of your status as a practicing parliamentarian. You may then apply to become a "certified parliamentarian," and, later on, a "certified professional parliamentarian." Certification is obtained by passing examinations and by documenting that you have been actively involved in the profession. See Chapter 9 for a more detailed discussion of AIP's credentialing program.

If you persist, you will eventually obtain formal credentials. However, as a general rule, you should not apply for certification until you have gained some experience as a parliamentarian for local organizations. Remember that your training to become a parliamentarian requires more than just reading books. Taking workshops and seminars and interacting with other aspiring parliamentarians will help, but even these will not complete your education. The "missing ingredient" is experience. There is no substitute for experience in the field. Read on.

Chapter 4
Your First Jobs, How to Begin

Having obtained the basic tools of your trade, you are now ready to begin work. All of your advance preparation is about to pay off. All you need to do now is put out the word that you are available and the high-paying jobs will roll in, right? Wrong!

Your choice as you will quickly discover, is between local organizations (which often do not have the resources to hire a parliamentarian), and large, well-funded organizations (which usually limit their search to parliamentarians with years of experience in the field). Since the well-funded organizations will usually not consider hiring a parliamentarian with no experience, you really have only one choice, and that is to start with small, local groups.

Your first jobs should not be taken to produce income, but to gain experience in the field. Following is a "road map" that has worked well for many professional parliamentarians.

1. Look in the right places.

    Many organizations that lack funding to hire professional parliamentarians will welcome the services of a volunteer. Since you have already begun your training in the field, you are more qualified than most volunteers, most of whom have never so much as opened a copy of *Robert's Rules*. Parent-Teacher Associations (PTAs) and Parent-Teacher Organizations (PTOs) are often willing to accept the services of a volunteer parliamentarian. Many service clubs, including Toastmasters, regularly have parliamentarians at their meetings and publish their own literature promoting the study of parliamentary procedure. Volunteer organizations such as the Junior Leagues promote the study of parliamentary procedure, and member Leagues often have member parliamentarians. Church organizations, garden clubs, social and athletic organizations, university faculty associations, student associations, and many others have used parliamentarians to help write bylaws, conduct elections, and run meetings.

You only need to look around in your community to find organizations where you can gain valuable experience. You should, however, be selective in choosing which organization(s) to serve. Some organizations will be much more valuable for your training than others.

2. Develop criteria for selecting your organization(s).

    Almost any organization that has bylaws will be happy to accept the services of a volunteer parliamentarian. You, however, should not necessarily "jump" at the first opportunity that appears. You are about the make a serious commitment to serve, and you need to ask yourself whether working for a given association will provide the kind of experience that you need. Suggested criteria for selecting an organization are:

    a. Are the governing documents of the organization coherent and well organized?

        If the documents need major revisions, you should recommend the services of a professional parliamentarian. Your first jobs should be with organizations that are basically well structured. At a later stage of your development you will seek organizations that need new bylaws, but first you want to deal with organizations that have a solid, comprehensible structure in place.

    b. Does the organization use parliamentary procedure?

        Some organizations pay "lip service" to parliamentary procedure, but don't really follow the rules. A few of the tell-tale clues that parliamentary procedure is not being followed are:

        The chair entertains extensive discussion while no motion is pending. Parliamentary procedure requires that a motion be moved, seconded, and stated by the chair before discussion is permitted.

        Discussion is not limited to one topic at a time, but tends to "ramble" over a number of different topics. Parliamentary procedure limits discussion to the pending question.

The same two or three favored speakers are recognized repeatedly by the chair while others are ignored. Parliamentary procedure requires that no one be recognized to speak a second time until everyone has had the opportunity to speak once.

Discussion is arbitrarily cut off by the chair, or upon demand of one person. Parliamentary procedure requires a two-thirds vote to stop debate.

c.   Will the presiding officer listen to the parliamentarian's advice in critical situations?

Some presiding officers have the unfortunate tendency of ignoring the parliamentarian, and you don't want to be in this situation. You should interview the presiding officer and find out how and when this person intends to consult with the parliamentarian. You could be embarrassed if your advice is not heeded at a critical moment. Try to find out just how committed the presiding officer is to maintaining order and ensuring that rules are followed. Also, find out whether this person listens to other advisers, or ignores them.

d.   .Are the meetings orderly?

Be sure to observe at least one or two meetings of the association that you are considering. Some organizations routinely turned their business meetings into a "circus" with personal insults, inappropriate language, and violation of the rules being the norm rather than the exception. Such groups probably won't follow your advice, and you will be wasting your time with them.

e.   Could your affiliation with this organization lead to future job opportunities?

This criterion might seem very selfish, but you will need contacts and references when you begin hunting for jobs that pay substantial fees. Look for positions that are likely to provide future contacts for you. A local association often will have a "parent organization" at the state level, and maybe even at the national level. A state organization may have many "sister organizations" in other states. The more connected your organization is with other groups, the more likely it will lead to future jobs for you. You will also be looking for letters of reference, so keep these considerations in mind when selecting your first volunteer jobs.

3. Select your organization(s) and stay with them for at least a year.

Once you have made your selection and have committed yourself to service, you should plan to stay with the organization(s) for a reasonable length of time. You will gradually become accustomed to working with the membership, and they will be accustomed to having you around to help ensure that procedures are consistently followed. It is not fair to you or to the membership to suddenly disappear. Normally, you should not leave in the middle of a president's one-year term. Give at least a month's notice before resigning your position, and try to time your resignation to coincide with the conclusion of the officers' term of office. You want to leave in the organization's good graces, preferably with at least two letters of reference.

The Art of Adapting

As you enter the "real world" of local organizations, you will quickly find that much of what you learned in books no longer applies. Each organization has its own culture, its own language and traditions, its unique way of communicating among members. You will now have to adapt what you have learned to the needs of the organization, and this process of "adapting" will gradually transform you from a novice into a practicing professional.

You may have learned from your parliamentary authorities, for example, that the customary way for a member to obtain recognition of the chair is to rise and say "Madam Chair" or "Mister Chair." The local bylaws, however, may state that the presiding officer is to be addressed as "Madam Chairperson." You should not, of course, argue with the bylaws. Language that has been placed in the bylaws must be adhered to, even if you personally disagree with that particular choice of words.

In other organizations, you may find that the bylaws are silent on the matter of addressing the chair, but the local custom is to say "Hey, Joe," or some such informal reference. The chair, who should normally begin the meeting with a single tap of the gavel, may pound the lectern several times. Further, members may have developed the habit of "calling the question" as a means of attempting to close debate.

All of these real-life situations pose challenges for the novice parliamentarian. You may be tempted to correct all of the errors at once, insisting right from the beginning that the parliamentary authority be followed in detail. Don't fall into this trap. The unfortunate outcome of being too rigid with the rules is that members may come to dislike parliamentary procedure in general, and parliamentarians in particular.

Instead of instant, radical reform of the membership, you may choose to accept the organization and its members as they are. It is important that, before you seek to change them, you learn about them and find out what their priorities are. Look for ways to improve communication, to ensure clarity in the proceedings, and to gradually educate the membership on the basic principles of democratic decision-making.

It may take months, perhaps even years, to bring an organization and its membership from a state of relative chaos to the orderly, well organized procedures described in the organization's parliamentary authority. Patience, however, is a key factor in working with the membership. You will need to develop a step-by-step plan for educating the membership on the basics of parliamentary procedure.

A Warning About Working Pro Bono

Your first jobs will usually not pay you a fee. Be careful, however, that you don't fall into the "trap" of not taking your job seriously just because you are not being paid. Even though you are not being paid in cash, the organization can provide you with valuable experience, references, and possible future contacts if you fulfill your responsibilities to the organization.

Some parliamentarians have made the mistake of assuming that, because they do not charge a fee, they need not prepare carefully for meetings. The reality is that every single time you serve as parliamentarian your reputation is "on the line." You will be held responsible for all of the advice that you give to the organization, whether or not you are paid for it.

It is not uncommon for ethics charges and lawsuits to be brought against parliamentarians who failed to prepare adequately for meetings or otherwise abused their position. The complaint, "I didn't even charge them anything" will not absolve you of your responsibility to the organization in your official capacity as parliamentarian. When you accepted the appointment, you made a pledge, in effect, to provide quality advice based upon your expertise, research, and best judgment.

It is important, therefore, that you look carefully before you commit your services to an organization and, once have accepted an appointment, stay with it at least to the conclusion of your presiding officer's term of office.

As a practicing novice, you are building a reputation that will follow you throughout your professional career. Many professional jobs are obtained by "word of mouth," as organizations communicate with each other about the experience they have had with their parliamentarians. Years after you have left the job, no one will remember whether or how much you were paid, but many people will remember the quality of service that you rendered.

Chapter 5
Preparing for Meetings
The parliamentarian's main work should be done
<u>outside</u> the meeting.[1] [Emphasis added.]

Occasionally, an organization will neglect to appoint a parliamentarian until one or two days prior to the meeting. The conscientious parliamentarian will refuse such an appointment, knowing that there is not time to prepare adequately. Keeping in mind that the parliamentarian will always be held accountable for advice rendered (regardless of the fee paid or not paid, and regardless of the time allowed for advance preparation), it is in the parliamentarian's best interest to accept only those jobs that allow time for the necessary preparation.

The parliamentarian's initial preparation should focus on (1) collection and study of key governing documents, (2) script preparation, (3) meeting with the president and vice president, and (4) physical setup.

Governing Documents

The parliamentarian's initial preparation consists of gathering all of the relevant documents and studying them in detail. Depending on the type of organization, applicable documents may include a certificate of incorporation, bylaws, standing rules, and the parliamentary authority. In addition to these documents, it is usually wise to read through two or three sets of past minutes.

As you read through the various governing documents, look for omissions, contradictions, and inconsistencies. These may help you spot "problem areas" before they actually become problems for the organization. They may also help you get to the root of long-festering problems that tend to reoccur. Part of your job is to alert the organization to any errors in the governing documents that may cause procedural problems.

In addition to the governing documents, you will require copies of the meeting notice, if any, the proposed agenda, and the minutes of the previous meeting. You should ensure that each meeting is properly noticed to the members. Pay particular attention to the notice of any special

---

[1] *Robert's Rules of Order Newly Revised*, 11th ed. (Da Capo Press, 2011), 466.

meeting, since this notice must specify the exact business to come before the meeting. The agenda, of course, may be amended before it is adopted, but you must be thoroughly familiar with the initial proposal. You also need to study the minutes of the previous meeting to ensure that any unfinished business that arises from these minutes is not overlooked.

Script Preparation

Another document that deserves close attention is the script. Not all organizations use scripts, but the presiding officer who has a script will usually be more confident and poised, and will make fewer errors in the use of parliamentary language. Some organizations prepare separate scripts for other key participants, such as the vice president, the secretary, the treasurer, and the chair of the bylaws committee.

The purpose of a script is to provide the exact language required for presiding and reporting to the assembly. Grammar should be thoroughly checked in advance. The correct pronunciation of proper names should be verified. Most importantly, the parliamentarian provides the correct use of parliamentary language throughout the script.

Most parliamentarians do not write scripts "from scratch," although a few do. When scripts are prepared by staff, the parliamentarian may be a key consultant in working through the language for amending bylaws, processing motions, and other procedural matters. Much of your advance preparation may consist of consulting with staff members who are writing the script. In any case, if there is a script, you should be thoroughly familiar with the content *before* the meeting starts.

The President and Vice President

You will certainly want to meet with the president, and probably the vice president as well, prior to your first meeting with the organization. The president needs to have a clear understanding of his or her role during meetings, i.e., adhering to the adopted agenda, recognizing speakers, processing motions, retaining control at all times, and so forth. Both the president and the vice president need to understand what happens when the president vacates the chair and the vice president becomes the presiding officer. Both of these individuals also need a clear understanding of your role as a key adviser during meetings.

In some situations, you will need to conduct formal "training sessions" for the president and vice president. If they have no background in parliamentary procedure, you will have to teach them how to construct and adopt an agenda, how to process a main motion, and how to handle amendments and other key motions in proper sequence. Your objective is not to make them experts in parliamentary procedure, but to bring them to the point where they can understand and apply the advice that you will be giving during meetings.

If a script is to be utilized, the president and vice president may need specialized training in the proper use of a script. They need to understand at what points they must adhere to the exact words of the script, and at what points they may, or should deviate from the script. Backup scripts may be written for special situations (such as an appeal) that require the presiding officer to deviate from the primary script.

When working with beginning presiding officers, it is almost always wise to recommend the use of a script. For some who are already skilled in the use of parliamentary language, an outline may suffice. The presiding officer, however, needs more than a "bare bones" agenda. Part of your job is to help the presiding officer discover and develop the necessary tools for presiding. These tools might include lists of names of members, dignitaries to be introduced, persons to be appointed to committees, early identification of potential problem areas, and similar items.

Physical Setup

The degree of control that the parliamentarian has over the physical set-up of the meeting varies widely from one organization to another. At a minimum, however, the parliamentarian needs to control his or her seating in relation to the presiding officer. Other officers and key staff will often compete for space in proximity to the presiding officer. At the time of hiring and signing an agreement, the parliamentarian must be insistent on close proximity to the presiding officer during business sessions. The presiding officer and parliamentarian must be close enough to shake hands without stretching. In no event should anyone be permitted to sit between the presiding officer and the parliamentarian.

Other aspects of the physical setup include the following:

1. How will other advisers be situated in relation to the presiding officer? The executive director may need to be close at hand for advice on substantive matters. Other officers are commonly seated at a head table in reasonably close proximity to the presiding officer.

2. Where will guests and nonmembers be seated? It may be important for these people to sit separately from voting members. It may also be important for these people to be seated where they can ask questions.

3. How many microphones will be required and where will these be located? It is usually wise to reserve one microphone for the exclusive use of the presiding officer. This ensures that no one will take control of the meeting away from the presiding officer. If the board of directors is seated on the dais, it may be necessary to have one or more "board mikes." It may also be necessary to have a microphone for reporting officers and committee chairs.

4. Some meetings have a special microphone designated for points of order and other priority motions that can interrupt. The parliamentarian should have a clear line of sight to this microphone, and should assist the presiding officer in determining what motions and discussion, if any, are in order from this microphone.

5. How will motion forms be distributed and collected? During large conventions, motion forms may be available at each microphone. Sometimes motion forms are located at a business table located in front of the dais. Once a motion form has been completed, a specific procedure for distributing copies should be implemented. It is essential that readable copies of the motion form go to the presiding officer, the secretary, and the parliamentarian.

6. How will votes be taken and reported? Seating arrangements can have a significant effect on the efficiency and fairness of counting votes. Aisles must be wide enough to allow the vote-counters to move freely and report results back to the presiding officer.

7. Where will the business table be located? This is frequently located directly in front of the dais, but may be off to a side. People working at the business table may occasionally need to communicate with the presiding officer. Many functions are performed at the

business table, such as distribution of motion forms, distribution of materials to microphone monitors, and distribution of minutes and announcements. The timer, the executive director, and other staff may be seated at this table. Counted votes may be tabulated at the business table and the results conveyed to the presiding officer.

One of the main functions of the physical setup is to enable to the presiding team to function smoothly. Chapter 6 will discuss problems of team coordination in more detail.

This page intentionally left blank.

Chapter 6
Being a Team Member

You may never have thought of the parliamentarian as a member of a "team." In reality, however, both the presiding officer and the parliamentarian are highly dependent on other key members of the presiding team. You should become acquainted with other team members as far in advance of the meeting as possible. It is important that other team members see you as a "partner." Use your verbal and nonverbal "people skills" to convey important messages to other team members. Messages that you do *not* want to convey to other team members include:

- I don't need your help.

- You must follow my instructions.

- My specialized knowledge of parliamentary procedure makes me "special" compared to other team members.

- My proximity to the presiding officer gives me authority over other team members.

Team members should be picking up signals from you to the effect that:

- We are all in this together.

- We all share a common goal, to help get the business of the assembly done as fairly and efficiently as possible.

- We are working together as equals, and no one of us is superior to other team members.

- My role is that of adviser, and I fully recognize the importance of other advisers who will require the attention of the presiding officer from time to time.

If you convey these positive messages of equality and cooperation to other team members, you will be more effective in your role as parliamentarian. You are likely to receive timely help from other team members that would not be given to a parliamentarian who stays aloof and maintains an attitude of superiority. Also, once you have established a bond of trust and cooperation with other team members, they are more likely to approach you for advice, and perhaps even formal training, that will lead to more effective job performance.

Now let's review the members of your team, which will vary in size and composition from one organization to another, and the unique function performed by each member.

The Presiding Officer

The position of presiding officer may, at various times, be performed by the president, the vice president, or the president-elect. It is important that you establish a working relationship with any person who may become an occupant of the chair. This relationship includes developing a system of communication that will work during meetings. Will your advice be limited to responding to direct questions? Or will you attempt to anticipate procedural problems and bring these to the attention of the presiding officer? The presiding officer needs to understand exactly what kind of advice you will provide, and how it will be given.

Advice may be given orally (by whispering), or silently (by use of a card system or nonverbal signal). It is up to you to work with the presiding officer to establish a system of advice that will be unobtrusive yet effective. Parliamentarians often become skilled in communicating with the presiding officer while members' attention is diverted away from the dais. If no script is available, the parliamentarian may need to provide correct parliamentary terminology. The presiding officer may also require guidelines to help decide when the parliamentarian should address the assembly directly to explain a technical procedure.

The Secretary

The most common error made by beginning secretaries is that they try to put too much into the minutes. The secretary needs to understand the difference between a transcript and a set of minutes. Secretaries are often appreciative of parliamentarians who advise them on what to include and what to omit from the minutes. Timely advice may result in shorter, better organized, and more coherent minutes.

Another responsibility of the secretary that should be clarified prior to the meeting is to keep a running record of pending motions. At any given point in the meeting, the presiding officer may ask the secretary to read the exact words of the immediately pending question, or a series of pending questions. To fulfill this responsibility, the secretary needs to be skilled in handling motion forms. The secretary's job becomes much more complex in the absence of motion forms. If motion forms are not used, the secretary must be adamant about receiving all motions and amendments *in writing*.

The Executive Director

In very large organizations, the "team leader" is often the executive director. This person hires the team and defines the exact responsibilities of each team member. Most executive directors understand the role of the parliamentarian as an expert on meeting procedures who provides advice to the presiding officer and others as needed. It is common practice for the parliamentarian to sit on one side of the presiding officer's lectern, and the executive director on the other side. With this arrangement, the executive director can provide advice on substantive matters that come before the assembly while the parliamentarian focuses on procedural advice.

It is important that the parliamentarian and the executive director develop a plan for dispensing advice. Too much advice given under stress can be confusing and distracting to a presiding officer. When the presiding officers requires assistance from two or more advisers, plan on taking "breaks" so that the presiding officer is not burdened with presiding responsibilities while receiving critical advice.

The Timer

The timer may be seated either on the dais or at the business table. The parliamentarian needs to find out how speeches are being timed and what kind of time signals are being given to the speaker and/or the presiding officer. Is timing limited to individual speeches, or is there also an overall limit on the time allowed for a single item on the agenda? Are points of order and points of information included in the timing? Is a vote included in the time? Are reports timed, or is only debate timed? How will speakers know when their time is up, and how will the presiding officer enforce time limits? If the timer is inexperienced, the parliamentarian may need to help clarify various aspects of keeping time.

The Attorney

Large associations often hire an attorney who advises on all matters involving legal documents and issues. Attorneys frequently do not attend meetings, but are available for consultation between meetings, and sometimes by phone during meetings. Whether or not the attorney is in attendance, this person is an important member of the team. The parliamentarian will sometimes be asked questions that have legal implications, and such questions should be immediately referred to the association attorney.

Other Staff

Large conventions often require the services of staff members who perform specialized functions. A spotter may be assigned to determine the order in which speakers were seeking to be recognized, and assist the presiding officer in ensuring that speakers are recognized in the proper order. Runners may deliver completed motion forms to the business table or dais, and may deliver written messages between the presiding officer and other team members. Microphone monitors may be assigned to each microphone to provide motion forms and assist members in gaining recognition by the presiding officer. Some organizations with limited staff appoint one member as floor manager to assist other members in writing motions, lining up speakers for debate, keeping up-to-date lists of nominees for office, and so forth.

The parliamentarian should develop a working relationship with all of these staff personnel. Be ready to respond to questions about the chair's recognition of speakers, the appropriate use of microphones in the hall, the distribution of motion forms, and related issues. You may occasionally require the services of a runner to get a message to the timer or a microphone monitor. Be careful not to treat these staff members as inferior to yourself. Remember that you are all part of the same team, and your objective is the same, that is, to move the business of the assembly forward as fairly and efficiently as possible.

Committee Chairs

You may never have considered committee chairs to be part of the presiding team, but they often perform key roles in the business of the assembly. All committee chairs need to know how to write a report, especially if the report contains specific recommendations for action by the assembly. Committees, which may require the services of a parliamentarian from time to time, include credentials, rules, tellers, bylaws, and many others. A meeting script may include the exact words to be spoken by each reporting committee chair.

The parliamentarian should cultivate a working relationship with the key committee chairs who will be active during the meeting. When a major election is scheduled, the parliamentarian may need to provide special training for the nominating committee and the tellers committee. When a bylaws revision is pending, the parliamentarian may need to consult frequently with the bylaws committee. Members frequently seek advice about the proper time to bring forth a motion, and the parliamentarian may advise members who wish to make motions pertaining to certain committee reports.

This page intentionally left blank.

Chapter 7
Working the Meetings

The portion of your work that most people observers can actually see is how you handle yourself during meetings. You know, of course, that more time was spent doing advance preparation than will be spent during the meeting itself. Keep in mind, however, that most members only get to see you during the meeting, and the way that you conduct yourself during meetings is an important measure of your success as a parliamentarian.

Last Minute Preparations

The fifteen to twenty minutes prior to the meeting should be planned in advance. If members need to consult with you, this probably should have been done earlier. Try to handle any last minute questions quickly because you need the time right before the meeting to focus on your job. Complex questions about procedure, if they were not raised well before the meeting, may need to be deferred to the period following the meeting if they are not resolved during the meeting itself. You cannot afford to become entangled in complex procedural questions during this important preparation time immediately before the meeting starts.

1. Arrange your tools carefully.

    Your primary attention immediately before any meeting is to be sure that the "tools of your trade" are immediately at hand, and organized so that you can access them as needed. Items that should be within easy reach include the meeting agenda, the minutes of the previous meeting, the parliamentary authority, bylaws, standing rules and special rules of order, special orders of the day, script(s), and signal cards if you plan to use these as a means of communication with the presiding officer.

    To be properly organized, you require "table space," so don't allow yourself to be squeezed too tightly among others at the head table. Arrive early and begin arranging your materials, using nonverbal cues to alert others that you need the space for arranging your materials properly. During the "heat" of decision-making, you will be glad that you took the time to ensure that all of your tools are readily at hand.

2. If microphones are used, check your "line of sight."

You need to be positioned so that you can hear and see what is going on during the meeting. This may require moving some of the microphones, or moving your seating position, to establish clear lines of sight with each microphone. If one of the microphones is designated for points of order and other motions that can interrupt, this microphone should usually be near the front of the room and easily visible to both the presiding officer and the parliamentarian.

If microphones are not used, you could have problems hearing some of the members. This makes it especially important that motions forms be used for all motions and amendments. You cannot afford to be in the position of guessing what members are trying to say.

3. Check the lighting and other aspects of the physical setup.

Much of the physical setup will not be within the control of the parliamentarian. In many cases, the setup was arranged in advance by a convention committee, or was set up by members well in advance. Nevertheless, you should be aware of any aspects of the physical setup that could cause problems in communication, and you can make your recommendations for changes for future meetings if it is not practical to make immediate changes.

Some of the factors that can cause distraction are:

a. Lighting. Some lighting setups are done primarily for video cameras rather than for the convenience of members. Harsh lighting of the dais may make it impossible for the presiding officer to see beyond the first two or three rows. Dim light can make it difficult for members to read their copies of the meeting agenda and any handouts that may be distributed during the meeting.

b.   Physical distance. The distance between the head table, the dais, and members can cause communication problems. Members may be so far removed from the dais that they cannot gain the chair's attention. If the dais is large, with many board members sitting out to the side of the main lectern, these people may have trouble gaining recognition. If guests are allowed to mix with the voting members, this may push some voting members too far to the rear of the room.

c.   Temperature control. Maintaining a comfortable temperature for all occupants of a large room is nearly impossible. The most common complaint heard at meetings is that the room is too cold. But, if the temperature is turned up, others can be seen taking off their jackets. The dais may be considerably warmer than other parts of the room because of heat from bright lights. Be prepared to "dress cool" in case the area around the dais is overheated.

d.   Note the location of your other team members and talk with as many of them as possible before the meeting begins. The time right before the meeting begins is an excellent time to ensure that other team members are "on the same page," i.e., they understand their job and understand the role that you will play during the meeting. If you plan to change your seating position at any point during the meeting (such as for the arrival of a guest speaker), be sure that other team members are alerted to this in advance.

e.   Check the distribution system for motion forms, meeting agendas, and other key documents that require distribution. Ensure that you will not be left "out of the loop" when important materials are distributed. You should be able to view the same materials that are being viewed by the membership. It is especially important that motions forms reach in you in a timely manner. Some parliamentarians routinely sort out the motions forms and hand them to the presiding officer.

During the Meeting

During the meeting your most important obligation is to stay consistently focused on procedures. You should not be concerned with the outcome of any vote, and under no circumstances should you try to influence a vote. While others are "waxing hot" on controversial issues, you should be calmly keeping an eye on the procedures. If observe procedures being violated, or anticipate procedural problems, it is your duty to help get the meeting back on track.

Most parliamentarians construct "ladders" of pending motions during meetings, placing the main motion at the bottom of the ladder, and any amendments, other subsidiary motions, and privileged motions higher up the ladder. Then, if the presiding officer leans over and asks, "Where are we?" the question can be answered with a simple reference to the ladder. The same techniques can be used to reply to a parliamentary inquiry which asks, "What are we voting on?" or "What are we supposed to be discussing?"

Remember that the presiding officer is dealing with members and issues, not procedures. This person is often totally dependent on you to ensure that discussion is conducted fairly and that the vote is taken properly. The nature of your job dictates that you must never be distracted from observing meeting procedures and ensuring that the proper procedures are followed.

You also have an obligation to remain physically "at your post," which is directly next to the presiding officer. Occasionally members will try to ask you a question in the middle of a meeting—they may even request that you step away from the dais briefly to respond to a question. Resist these temptations. No matter how pressing the issue, your place is beside the presiding officer. If something of an emergency nature arises that requires immediate attention, it is possible for the presiding officer to declare a brief recess. But if no recess is declared, you must remain at your post.

As you become more familiar with the adopted parliamentary authority, you will learn how to look up answers to questions very quickly during meetings. The parliamentarian should always have the parliamentary authority at hand, and should be able to locate answers to simple procedural questions in a few moments, and to develop facility in using the parliamentary authority. In some situations, members will accept your advice without question, but in other situations they want to see the "quote from the book" that justifies a given procedure.

The advice that you give during meetings should normally not be limited to responding to direct questions. Part of your job is to anticipate procedural problems before they arise. If, for instance, you believe that the meeting is in danger of losing a quorum, you should call this to the attention of the chair. If members' discussion is beginning to diverge from the immediately pending question, don't hesitate to inform the chair. If requests for information are starting to become discussion (which is usually true of a five-part question), you should help the chair curb this abuse before it gets out of hand. If you keep your attention consistently focused on procedures, you will find many ways to become a proactive parliamentarian, taking preventative steps to ensure an orderly meeting.

This page intentionally left blank.

Chapter 8
Follow Up

When the final gavel falls, your work for the meeting is done. However, a conscientious parliamentarian will usually follow up with a number of things that need to be done, especially if you will be doing future work for the same organization. Follow up measures may include any or all of the following.

Compliment the Team

Even if some things went wrong during the meeting, you should compliment team members. Remember that this was not just your individual effort, nor the efforts of many individual people; it was a team effort in which, hopefully, the "whole" was more than the sum of its parts.

Begin with the presiding officer. You are the one seated closest to this person, and he or she could use a little praise, especially after a lengthy, contentious meeting. To some, it may look like you are being condescending in offering praise, but this misses the point. The position of presiding officer is essentially a lonely position that requires an enormous amount of poise, confidence, and restraint to be successful. Throughout the meeting, you should note both the strengths and weaknesses of the presiding officer. The time immediately following the meeting is when you should highlight strengths, perhaps even congratulating the presiding officer for having performed so well in a difficult situation. Discussion of any aspects of presiding that require improvement can wait.

Why should you speak to the presiding officer as soon as the gavel falls? Partly, you want to subtly remind this person that the successful result of the meeting was due to a team effort, and you are part of that team. Be sure to compliment the presiding officer on his coordination of the team. This person is, after all, the team leader, and much of the success or failure of the team depends on the leader's ability to recognize and utilize the various functions performed by team members. If you feel that the presiding officer utilized especially well the services of the parliamentarian or any other team members, say so.

As time permits, speak to other team members before they leave the meeting. Compliment the vice president who assumed the chair with dignity and poise at an unexpected moment. Compliment the secretary who was always alert and ready to read aloud the exact words of pending motions. Compliment a committee chair whose report was especially clear and well organized, with specific recommendations placed at the end of the report. Compliment the chair of the sergeant-at-arms committee or the microphone monitors who helped maintain order during heated debate. These compliments are not condescending; they are an honest effort on your part to build and foster team coordination which is essential to any well run meeting.

Have a Debriefing Session

If possible, meet with the presiding officer to discuss anything that went wrong in the meeting. The debriefing session should normally not be held immediately after the meeting, but, if possible, within the two or three days following. Were there any problems with the script? Should the type be larger? Are additional back-up scripts needed for special situations? Were speakers actually recognized in proper order? Were there any problems with handling points of order, appeals, or substitute motions?

How effectively did the presiding officer and the parliamentarian communicate during the meeting? Should the parliamentarian use more or fewer signals to get the attention of the presiding officer? Did the presiding officer get confused because of too much advice coming simultaneously from different people? Were more "breaks" needed to reduce confusion? Did the parliamentarian speak directly to the assembly too much, or not enough?

Were motion forms handled in the best way possible? Did the presiding officer always have up-to-date information on which motions were pending, and motions that were waiting to be introduced? Were key speakers identified at the appropriate time? Were members of the assembly always clear on the status of pending amendments?

Were staff members fully aware of their respective roles as members of the presiding team? If not, a special workshop for team members may be required. Microphone monitors, sergeants-at-arms, runners, spotters, floor managers, and other team members should all understand exactly what their responsibilities are and how their efforts will complement and mesh with the efforts of the entire team.

Was the parliamentarian sufficiently available to other team members as well as to members of the assembly? If there were complaints that the parliamentarian was not accessible, perhaps "parliamentarian hours" should be established prior to the next meeting. Setting a definite time and place when the parliamentarian will be available to speak privately to anyone seeking procedural advice is an excellent method of facilitating communication. In most cases, consultation times should be set during the two or three hours preceding the meeting.

Some parliamentarians have developed evaluation forms to be completed by the presiding officer and other team members. These forms provide valuable feedback to the parliamentarian, and are the basis for developing guidelines for future meetings. If member evaluations of the meeting are available, these should also be reviewed by the parliamentarian.

Build Your File

Bear in mind, especially during the early years of your practice, that you must build a file of references. Any time that you have done an especially good job, be sure to follow up by asking key people for a letter of reference, or ask for permission to use the person's name as a future reference. If you are truly effective during meetings, chances are good that your reputation will spread by word-of-mouth. However, there will be many other situations in which you will apply for a job to parties who know nothing of you or your reputation. It is therefore essential that you build a file of letters of reference, and also names of people who would be willing to write a letter for you when called upon. All of this requires time, effort, and organization, but building your file is the part that you owe yourself.

Letters of reference are most commonly written by the executive director or president who hired you. Other possible sources include key committee chair (such as the chair of a bylaws committee who consulted with you during a bylaws revision) and members who sought your advice during a particularly contentious meeting. Any team members with whom you worked closely may write letters of reference for you.

As your experiences multiply and spread to other organizations, you should also develop and maintain an updated resume or "bio." Some parliamentarians maintain their bio on their professional website; others print it out on letterhead stationery or a printable brochure. Whatever form your bio takes, it is essential that your potential clients know about the successful experiences you have had as a practicing parliamentarian.

Evaluating Success

Team members often evaluate the success or failure of a meeting in terms of outcomes. If the "right" people got elected, the meeting was a success; if the "wrong" people got elected, the meeting was a failure. If the dues proposal was adopted, the meeting was a success; it the proposal was defeated, the meeting was a failure. If the bylaws revision was adopted with only a few minor amendments, the meeting was a success; it the revision failed, then the meeting was a failure. The parliamentarian should never be a party to this type of evaluation.

Another error in evaluation occurs when people assume that, if the meeting was successful, everyone should leave the meeting room feeling satisfied and happy. Parliamentary procedure, however, does not utilize decision making by consensus. Rather it seeks to discover the will of the majority, and to implement the decisions of the majority. It also endeavors to ensure that all points of view are heard, and that minority rights are not violated. When differences of opinion become polarized and fully articulated, it is inevitable that some people on the losing side of an issue will leave the meeting less than satisfied. Remember that your job is not to make everyone happy; rather, your job is to promote democratic decision making in which everyone has an equal chance to be heard and votes are fairly taken.

The following questions provide guidelines for evaluating the success or failure of a meeting:

- Were key issues identified and placed on the agenda?

- Were issues addressed one at a time, and adequately considered before voting?

- Did everyone have an equal opportunity to speak?

- Was the meeting conducted in such a way that no one individual or clique was allowed to dominate the discussion?

- Did the business of the assembly move forward at a reasonable pace, without being obstructed by any minority group?

- Were procedures understood by everyone, and did the business proceed in an orderly fashion?

- Was the will of the assembly discovered and implemented?

If the answer to all of the above is *yes,* you have been a key participant in a very successful meeting. Members may occasionally complain that a meeting was "boring." Your job, however, is not to provide entertainment. If the business of the assembly was accomplished fairly and efficiently, you have done your job. No one can ask more of a parliamentarian.

This page intentionally left blank.

Chapter 9
Moving Up in the Profession

At some point in your career, you will want to begin "networking" with other parliamentarians. The best way to do this is through a professional association such as the American Institute of Parliamentarians. A huge advantage of networking is that you can find out how other parliamentarians have resolved the kinds of problems that you will face with your clients. Networking will also enable you to keep up with the latest literature and developments in the field.

Specialized workshops, seminars, and practicums are offered for parliamentarians every year. Some of these help to apply the principles of parliamentary procedure to special settings such as condominium associations, church organizations, or legislative bodies. Some will focus on the legal aspects of court decisions that affect the practice of parliamentary procedure. Others will focus on technological developments and how parliamentarians can maximize their use of technology to assist clients. Still others will review basic skills of parliamentary procedure for beginning parliamentarians.

Once you become a member of AIP, you will quickly discover that there are various "levels" of membership. When you first join the organization, you will be considered a "regular member." Regular members are often students of parliamentary procedure, and many do not advance beyond this type of membership. Some join because they were recently elected to an office in a local organization, and they want to learn more about how to carry out their responsibilities. Others have witnessed meetings that were poorly run, and want to know the correct way of handling meeting procedures. Although regular membership is commendable, you, as an aspiring professional parliamentarian, will want to move up in the profession and gain credentials that can be used with future clients.

The Credentialing Process

AIP offers two levels of credentials: Certified Parliamentarian (CP) and Certified Professional Parliamentarian (CPP). Either of these will help you gain clients, but your ultimate goal should be attain the highest level of membership (CPP) that is available. CPs and CPPs may also earn another credential as a Certified Parliamentarian-Teacher (CP-T) or as a Certified Professional Parliamentarian-Teacher (CPP-T).

There are two basic requirements to become a CP. You must accumulate "service points" based on your experience in the field and you must pass a written examination. Your achievement of the required number of service points, after approval by the AIP Accrediting Department, will be presented to the board of directors by the accrediting director when you are considered for reclassification as a Certified Parliamentarian. You may obtain the current list of requirements for service points directly from AIP Headquarters.

The written examination is comprehensive and will test your knowledge of several different parliamentary authorities. Information about the parliamentary authorities on which the exams are based, the availability of written examinations, and the rules for these examinations may also be obtained from the AIP Headquarters office.

Some novice parliamentarians are anxious to take an examination and become certified immediately after joining AIP. It is wise, however, to allow adequate time to obtain experience in the field. You should also supplement your private studies with attendance at workshops, seminars, and practicums taught by professional parliamentarians. If you try to "rush" the process, you invite failure. Give yourself time to grow and mature so that, when you do obtain your reclassification as a CP, you will be fully prepared to practice as a professional.

Preparing for Written Examinations

Don't assume that, just because you read several parliamentary authorities, you are ready to take an examination. Examination skills are something that you must learn separately. If you are a recent high school or college graduate, chances are that you have retained many of your test-taking skills. If, however, you have been not been involved in any formal schooling for more than three or four years, you may need to sharpen up your skills for taking examinations.

You can begin your studies with the simple principle of "overlearning" the material. This principle states simply that, if you study for questions that are more difficult than those you expect to see on the examination, the actual examination questions will appear easy by comparison. Make and grade your own quizzes. When making up the quizzes, don't write down the pages where the correct answers can be found. Then, grade the quiz by looking up each answer separately. You'll be surprised at how much material you retain by this "active learning" process.

You need not be completely surprised by the kinds of questions that will appear on the examination. Obtain a copy of the *AIP Study Manual* (2013) from the AIP bookstore, which is accessible on the AIP website. Studying the questions in this book is an excellent way to prepare for your examination.

If you visit a college bookstore, you will readily find books on how to study for examinations. These books also have helpful tips for taking tests, such as answering all of the "easy" questions first, then going back to deal with the more difficult questions.

Preparing for Oral Examinations

If you are a candidate for reclassification to CPP, you will be required to take an oral examination. Whereas a written examination tests your knowledge of specific facts, the oral examination goes beyond the facts and attempts to find out how you are likely to perform as a professional. For this examination, you will need to see relationships among the various parliamentary authorities. You will also have to draw from your own experiences to explain how various complex, real-life situations might be resolved.

The manner in which you present yourself and your ability to articulate concepts clearly are the "key" to passing an oral examination. If you are not accustomed to speaking in public, this might be an excellent time to take a workshop or course in basic public speaking skills. Poise and self-confidence do count heavily in taking an oral examination. In preparation for the oral examination, you should get plenty of rest, eat well, and dress appropriately. You want to be at your best and appear professional when you appear before the examining committee and the AIP members observing the examination.

Because the oral examination consists partly in a presiding demonstration, then you need to practice your presiding skills. This part of the examination puts you "in the shoes" of the presiding officer with whom you will be working in the field. During the examination, you are forced to make quick decisions without the aid of a parliamentarian to assist you. This tests your ability to perform under pressure. As a professional in the field, you will encounter numerous "pressure" situations in which tempers wax hot, and you will be expected to be a calming influence. The oral examination is partly a learning experience in staying calm while under pressure.

Retaking Examinations

If you do not pass your written or oral examination the first time, don't be discouraged. Many excellent professional parliamentarians did not pass on their first try. In the case of written examinations, no one need ever know that you even took the examination unless you yourself reveal this information. The oral examination is, by its very nature, public, so there is no way that you can hide the fact that you didn't pass the first time. Just keep in mind that many parliamentarians do not pass the first time. Years after you have become a CP or CPP, few if any will remember that you took the examination more than once, and taking the exam more than once won't have any effect on your well-earned credentials.

Gathering Your Tools

Once you have obtained your CP or CPP credentials, you must ensure that you have the necessary tools to pursue your chosen profession. Your tool kit will probably include business cards, letterhead stationery, brochures for mailing, a website, and an e-mail address. You can view other parliamentarians' websites by using any of the available search engines on your computer and typing in "parliamentarian" or "parliamentary procedure." You can easily find sample biographies and other material on these websites, which you can use to model your own website.

Unless you are unusually well connected with clients, you should consider joining a referral service such as that offered by AIP. Referral services typically charge a fee, but this a necessary business expense for many parliamentarians.

Other tools that you may find useful include a laptop computer, a cell phone, special luggage for carrying your papers, books, and other paraphernalia. You will want to choose carefully which tools to carry with you for certain client organizations. Given the status of the airlines today, there are definite advantages to "traveling light," and you should plan on extensive travel if you want to be truly professional.

Chapter 10
You and Your Clients

When you first enter the job market, you will find a few surprises. It probably should not surprise you to discover that many people who respond to your advertising are merely looking for free advice. Whether or not you are willing to provide free advice is entirely your choice, but always remember that you will be held responsible for any advice that you give, even if it is given free of charge. Telephone inquiries, with no opportunity to review any of the organization's governing documents, are especially dangerous. You may find yourself being misquoted even when you gave good advice. Or, you may find that the advice you gave was based on hearing only one side of the story when there were two or more sides to be heard.

When doing your job search, you will also discover that most organizations that are seriously interested in hiring a parliamentarian prefer to interview several applicants before making a decision. This should not discourage you. You may need to go through several interviews before landing your "perfect" long-term client. You do, however, need to develop interview skills. If you are not used to being interviewed, you should visit bookstores and find the most up-to-date resources on interview techniques. Your interview skills, or lack of them, may be a decisive factor in the organization's choice of a parliamentarian.

Choosing Clients

When applying for jobs, remember that not only is the client choosing a parliamentarian, but you also have an active role to play in choosing a client. Before applying for a job, you should do research on the organization's history and its previous parliamentarians, if any. Your initial examination of the organization's governing documents may convince you that this is not the organization for you.

If you find that the organization meets at a different location every year, and always hires the parliamentarian who lives closest to the meeting, this tells you that you have no chance of a long-term commitment.

If the organization has a history of frequently hiring and firing parliamentarians, try to find out the cause. Also, you may find that an organization has a history of paying very low fees, and this may or may not be of interest to you.

Job Opportunities

Probably the single type of position that is most frequently sought by parliamentarians is that of convention parliamentarian. Convention parliamentarians may be hired for a single convention or for a period of continuous service that may last a year or longer. Many experienced parliamentarians have chosen to limit their practice to long-term clients who retain their services for conventions as well as for teaching workshops, meeting with the board of directors and key committees, and providing other services. There is much less risk involved in working for a stable, long-term client than in short-term situations.

Parliamentarians should beware of organizations that do not hire parliamentarians except in temporary "crisis" situations. Ideally, the professional parliamentarian is looking for the type of position where potential crisis situations can be anticipated and brought under control before they "mushroom" into a full-blown crisis. Parliamentarians who regularly accept short-term appointments in crisis situations should probably be charging very high fees because of the high risks involved and the extra work involved in attempting to rescue an organization from the consequences of its past mistakes.

Of course, there are many other opportunities in the job market other than that of convention parliamentarian. Some are hired as "floor parliamentarians" to represent the interests of certain constituencies during a convention (assuming that a convention parliamentarian has already been hired to work on the dais). Some parliamentarians are hired as bylaw consultants and never attend a meeting. Some work as parliamentary consultants to attorneys. Some specialize in writing parliamentary opinions and never meet the client face-to-face. Some focus on teaching workshops in parliamentary procedure. Some are hired specifically to preside over meetings if this is permitted by the assembly or required in the organization's bylaws.

Charging Fees

Parliamentarians are always fascinated to find out the fees charged by other parliamentarians. In truth, many factors affect the fees that organizations will pay their parliamentarians and other consultants. The geographic area is often an important factor. A convention held in Washington, D.C., or New York City is likely to command a much higher fee than one held in a small town. The organization's finances are another important variable. Some are able to pay much more than others, and some are willing to pay "top dollar" to attract the best talent.

Another variable, of course, is the parliamentarian's background and experience. Large conventions are usually looking for parliamentarians with extensive education and experience. You should be willing to work for smaller fees if you are just beginning in the profession, and your fees will usually be substantially higher after you have worked extensively in the field.

A major variable that is often overlooked in determining fees is the parliamentarian's willingness to accept certain fees. Some parliamentarians who enjoy their work and are looking only for supplemental income are willing to work for very low fees. Others will not consider working unless they are paid "top dollar." There are no universal guidelines that specify how much a parliamentarian should be paid. It is up to you to decide what you are willing to work for, and it is up to your client to decide whether the amount you are asking is acceptable.

One approach to setting fees is to find out what the previous parliamentarian was paid. Although this amount may not match your expectation, it is your best indication of what the client organization has been accustomed to paying. It may also be close to the limit of what the organization is able and willing to pay.

Contracts and Agreements

Regardless of the fee to be paid, the written agreement between you and your client is critically important. Even if you do not charge a fee, you need some kind of agreement in writing about the services that you are expected to provide. Your written agreement should specify travel expenses that will be paid by the client. It also may specify certain conditions of your work, such as that you will be seated next to the presiding officer during meetings. As far as possible, the agreement should state exactly what kinds of services you will provide and the dates on which you will provide these services.

Some parliamentarians have contracts that are renewable on an annual basis. A contract may provide for services in connection with a convention and also provide for teaching workshops, attending board meetings and selected committee meetings, consulting on bylaws and other governing documents, and consulting on the writing of scripts. A sample contract agreement appeared in the October 1991 issue of the *Parliamentary Journal,* published by AIP.

The Member Parliamentarian

Many organizations routinely appoint one of their own members to serve as parliamentarian. If you are offered such an appointment, you should be aware that you will be giving up most of your membership rights. You will no longer have the right to debate issues, and you may never vote except on a ballot vote. More importantly, you must completely "divorce" yourself from substantive issues, and you must not be concerned with the outcome of any vote. As parliamentarian, your attention must be focused entirely on procedures. This is a challenge that some members can do successfully. Others, however, especially those who have been outspoken on controversial issues, may find it extremely difficult to avoid participating in the deliberations.

Protecting Yourself

In today's litigious society, there is no such thing as practicing a profession without risk. You can, however, take some of these common sense measures to protect yourself against lawsuits and ethics charges:

1. When writing a parliamentary opinion, always state that the opinion is based solely on the documents that were provided to you. This protects you from charges that may arise from your ignorance of the existence of certain documents.

2. Be sure that your advice is always referred to as a "parliamentary opinion," and not as a legal opinion. Parliamentarians must be vigilant that their advice is never construed as legal advice. Even

lawyers who practice as parliamentarians go to great lengths to distinguish between parliamentary advice and legal advice.

3. If you have a written contract with your organization, you may consider including a clause that requires the organization to assume liability for any lawsuits arising from your parliamentary advice.

Low-cost, group liability insurance for parliamentarians has been a primary objective of the profession for years. A few parliamentarians have purchased liability insurance individually, but premiums are high. Buy low-cost, group liability insurance if it is available.

This page intentionally left blank.

Chapter 11
Pay Back

Having established yourself as a practicing member of the profession, you should realize that the profession has helped you attain your goals in many ways. You probably learned parliamentary procedure not just from books, but by interacting with members of the profession in workshops, seminars, and practicums. You may have benefited from instructors who volunteered their time to help prepare you for entering the profession. When building your library, you borrowed heavily from others who have shared their experience and wisdom by writing articles and books. The credentialing program that enabled you to attain the CP or CPP (and possibly the T) reclassification was staffed by volunteer members of the profession. You may also have utilized the services of a referral service to obtain clients. Thus, at every step of the way, you were dependent upon the help of other members of the profession.

The question then arises whether you owe anything to your profession, and hopefully you will immediately understand that you do indeed owe much to those who have helped you along the way. Listed below are some of the ways in which you can repay your debt to the profession. The good news is that, by helping to advance your profession, you are also helping yourself. Collectively, parliamentarians can do much more together than any of them can do individually. Here, then, are some suggestions on how you can give "payback" to your profession.

Maintain active membership in the profession.

Active membership in the profession is an essential ingredient of pay back. You will have to pay dues, but you will receive a great deal in return. Your membership in AIP enables to you attend and vote in chapter meetings, regional conferences, and annual sessions. You will receive the *Parliamentary Journal* and the *Communicator* to keep you up-to-date with developments in the profession. Active membership is the first step that opens the door to many other types of service and opportunities in the profession.

Some members prefer to belong to only one organization, such as AIP. Others prefer "multiple membership" in several associations. Whether you join one or several organizations is your choice. The important thing is to maintain active membership in the profession.

Study the governing documents of the profession.

You can obtain a copy of AIP's Membership Directory directly from the AIP website. In addition to membership and AIP leadership, the directory also contains the AIP Action Program, the Bylaws, Standing Orders, Code of Ethics, and Rules for the Disposition of Ethics Complaints. Those documents can also be obtained individually from the AIP website.

The Action Program is probably the most important document, because it states the direction that the profession is headed. You should study this in detail to determine in which areas you can be most helpful.

A working knowledge of the governing documents, including the bylaws and standing orders will be important for your attendance and participation in any AIP business meetings.

The Code of Ethics, jointly adopted by the American Institute of Parliamentarians (AIP) and the National Association of Parliamentarians (NAP) in 2001, sets forth the minimum standards of ethical conduct expected of all members of the parliamentary profession.

As an active member of the profession, you should familiarize yourself with all of these documents early in your career. It is especially important for you to figure out what you can do to help implement the Action Program.

Recruit new members.

You may be surprised to learn that many people still do not know about the existence of AIP and other parliamentary organizations. You can help make people aware that these organizations do exist, and that they are very helpful in providing qualified parliamentarians and lists of materials for sale. At every opportunity, you should suggest the possibility of membership. The profession needs a constant inflow of new members to survive, and you can help "spread the word."

Attend educational events sponsored by the profession.

As a CP or CPP, you will be required to attend at least one major educational event every seven years, as a form of continuing education. But, even without this requirement, you should attend as many workshops, seminars, and practicums as your budget will permit.

It is a good practice to set aside a portion of your earnings specifically for this purpose. By attending and participating, you will support your profession at the same time that you are helping yourself through advanced education.

Prepare to teach.

There are many opportunities for teaching in the parliamentary profession. Teaching for client organizations is a common practice of professional parliamentarians. There are also many opportunities to teach other parliamentarians within the profession. Before you accept teaching assignments, however, you should prepare yourself to teach. You will need specific teaching skills, and if you do not have a background in education, you would be wise to enroll for AIP's Teacher Certification Course. Passing this course is a requirement for obtaining the Teacher credential, and the course will give you the basic skills that you need to teach beginning level workshop in parliamentary procedure for your client organizations. With experience, you can then move to higher levels of teaching at various AIP gatherings.

Do volunteer work for the profession.

Most of the work of promoting the parliamentary profession is done by volunteers who are "repaying their debt." The opportunities for service are almost unlimited. You can begin at the local level by joining an AIP chapter and contributing to the educational programs. At the national level of AIP, there are many opportunities to teach, serve on committees, and write for publication. Eventually you may run for the board of directors, or accept an appointment to assist with the accrediting program.

Opportunities often arise when they are least expected. As you network with other professionals and attend meetings, keep alert to the most pressing needs of the profession. It is only a matter of time, usually a very short time, before you find your "niche" and become a contributing volunteer worker.

Once you have done all of the above, you should congratulate yourself. You are now a full-fledged active member of the parliamentary profession. You are may now proceed to build your list of clients and travel extensively to promote AIP's mission: "to work for the improvement of parliamentary procedure to the end that decisions are made by parliamentary means rather than by violence or by dictatorial actions, and that mankind will learn to live in peace through effective implementation of sound democratic principles."

Parliamentary Authorities and Texts

Cannon, Hugh. *Cannon's Concise Guide to Rules of Order*. Houghton Mifflin Company, 1995.

Demeter, George. *Demeter's Manual of Parliamentary Law and Procedure*. Blue Book Ed. Little, Brown and Company, 1969.

Education Department, American Institute of Parliamentarians. *Fundamentals of Parliamentary Law and Procedure*. 4th ed. American Institute of Parliamentarians, 2014.

Phifer, Gregg (ed.) *Readings in Parliamentary Law*. Kendall/Hunt Publishing Company, 1992.

Riddick, Floyd M. and Miriam M. Butcher. *Riddick's Rules of Procedure*. Charles Scribner's Sons, 1985.

Robert, Henry M. *Robert's Rules of Order Newly Revised*. 11th ed. Ed. Sarah C. Robert. Da Capo Press, 2011.

AIP, *American Institute of Parliamentarians Standard Code of Parliamentary Procedure*. McGraw-Hill, 2012.

Articles in the AIP *Parliamentary Journal*
by M. Eugene Bierbaum

- "Parliamentary Manuals as Texts," July 1972.

- "Routes to Learning Parliamentary Procedure," July 1975.

- "The Role of the Presiding Officer," April 1978.

- "AIP's Accrediting Program," July 1981.

- "Bob English's AIP," January, April, July, and October 1983.

- "A Working Model for Parliamentarian-Client Relationships," October 1991.

- "The Adherence of Motions," October 1992.

- "Joint Code of Ethics: One Step in the Right Direction," July 2002.

- "The Ethics of Giving Parliamentary Advice," July 2003.

- "How to Respond to an Ethics Complaint," April 2005.

- "Teaching Principles," April 2006.

- "Bob English's AIP," October 2008.

- "The First AIP Practicum," October 2008.

- "AIP's Niche," April 2009.

- "How Much Should We Charge?" October 2009.

- "Ethical Parameters for Parliamentarians," April 2011.

- "Robert W. English Lecture," January, 2014.

Made in the USA
Las Vegas, NV
15 April 2024

88730412R00044